PUBLIC SERVICE

The Quiet Crisis

Paul A. Volcker

American Enterprise Institute for Public Policy Research

PUBLIC SERVICE:
THE QUIET CRISIS

The Francis Boyer Lectures on Public Policy

PUBLIC SERVICE:
THE QUIET CRISIS

Paul A. Volcker

American Enterprise Institute for Public Policy Research

Distributed by arrangement with

UPA, Inc.
4720 Boston Way
Lanham, MD 20706
3 Henrietta Street
London WC2E 8LU, England

ISBN 0-8447-1385-6

Printed in the United States of America

American Enterprise Institute
1150 Seventeenth Street, N.W., Washington, D.C. 20036

THE
FRANCIS BOYER LECTURES
ON PUBLIC POLICY

The American Enterprise Institute initiated the Francis
Boyer Lectures on Public Policy in 1976 to examine the
relationship between business and government in American society. The lectures are made possible by an endowment from the SmithKline Beckman Corporation in
memory of Mr. Francis Boyer (1893–1972), the late chairman of the board of the corporation and a distinguished
business leader for many decades.

The lecture is given annually by an eminent thinker
who has developed notable insights on the relationship
between the nation's private and public sectors. It is intended to illuminate central issues of public policy in contemporary America and contribute significantly to the dialogue by which the public interest is served.

The Francis Boyer lecturer is selected by the American Enterprise Institute's Council of Academic Advisers.
Lecturers may come from any walk of life—the academy,
the humanities, public service, science, finance, the media,
business, or industry. The man or woman delivering the
lecture is not necessarily a professional scholar, government official, or business leader. The principal considerations determining the selection are the quality and
appositeness of the lecturer's thought rather than his or
her formal qualifications.

The Francis Boyer Lecture is delivered in Washington, D.C., at the conclusion of the American Enterprise Institute's annual Policy Conference. These several days of seminars bring together government policy makers, business leaders, and scholars for the purpose of exploring the major policy problems facing the United States and the world.

Paul A. Volcker, the recipient of the 1987 Francis Boyer Award, was chosen in recognition of his many contributions to domestic and international economic policy during the past twenty-five years and for the qualities of intellect, judgment, and leadership he has exhibited throughout his career. After completing his education at Princeton, Harvard, and the London School of Economics, Mr. Volcker joined the Federal Reserve Bank of New York as a staff economist in 1952, remaining there until 1957 when he joined the Chase Manhattan Bank. From 1962 to 1965 he served as director of financial analysis at the U.S. Treasury Department, then returned to the Chase as a vice president until 1969, when President Nixon appointed him under secretary of the Treasury for monetary affairs, where he served until 1974. During this period he was the principal U.S. negotiator in the development of a new international monetary system replacing the fixed exchange rate system established after World War II.

In 1975 Mr. Volcker returned to the Federal Reserve Bank of New York as its president, serving until August 1979 when President Carter appointed him the chairman of the Board of Governors of the Federal Reserve System. In his two remarkable terms as Federal Reserve chairman (being reappointed by President Reagan in 1983) he achieved extraordinary stature and influence within the U.S. Congress, two administrations, and domestic and international financial circles. His firm resolve in the pursuit of monetary stability was widely regarded as the decisive element in overcoming the double-digit inflation that had severely handicapped the American economy in the 1970s and that had seemed a nigh permanent condition by the end of the decade.

After his retirement from the Federal Reserve in August 1987, Mr. Volcker became chairman of the National Commission on the Public Service, turning his attentions to a subject that had increasingly concerned him during his own years of public service—the problems of attracting and retaining talented individuals for careers in the federal government. Mr. Volcker's Boyer Lecture, *Public Service: The Quiet Crisis,* is devoted to this issue. The American Enterprise Institute is very pleased to publish this fine addition to its Francis Boyer Lecture series.

CHRISTOPHER C. DEMUTH
President
American Enterprise Institute
for Public Policy Research

Francis Boyer Award Recipients

1977   *Gerald R. Ford*
1978   *Arthur F. Burns*
1979   *Paul Johnson*
1980   *William J. Baroody, Sr.*
1981   *Henry A. Kissinger*
1982   *Hanna Holborn Gray*
1983   *Alan Walters*
1984   *Robert H. Bork*
1985   *Jeane J. Kirkpatrick*
1986   *David Packard*
1987   *Paul A. Volcker*

INTRODUCTION

It is a great pleasure indeed to introduce the Francis Boyer lecturer for 1987.

Paul Volcker is surely one of the outstanding public figures of our time. His record of public service is exemplary. His dedication to the public interest, in contrast to his personal needs, is truly remarkable. He has set a new, or perhaps has reminded us of a very old, standard for personal conduct in a dazzling age filled with all sorts of financial opportunity.

To the extent that Paul Volcker has become a legendary figure, many myths have arisen about him. Let me dispose of them quickly: Paul does not get his suits from Goodwill. He does not smoke nickel cigars—anymore. He never actually pinched a penny and has never, ever been seen carrying the punchbowl away from the party.

Let me report a personal incident to underscore his awesome powers of concentration on the task at hand. One day we were discussing some compelling aspect of monetary policy, when one of his notoriously smelly cigars landed in the wastebasket. Paul was oblivious to the smoke that began to engulf his office. He continued to make his point to a polite representative of the Reagan administration. Finally I interrupted him and put out the conflagration. Later on I had second thoughts. If word of my action got out, my supply-side friends might never forgive me.

On a somewhat more serious note, the essence of

central banking has been described as the ability to apply the brakes without throwing the passengers through the windshield. For those of us who are passengers on the Volcker Express, Paul's enduring accomplishment was unwinding escalating double-digit inflation while providing a legacy of sustainable economic growth. Paul, this nation is in your debt; but, like British consols, it may never be paid.

With a slight sense of guilt, I remind you of our first conversation after I left the Treasury in 1972. I was telling you of my early success on the lecture circuit, but you interrupted me with words I will never forget: "Murray, all I see are dollar signs dancing in your eyes. Remember, we were trained for the public service."

Today, as your friends and admirers, we salute you for your uniquely distinguished public service. AEI is truly honored by your acceptance of our invitation to give the Boyer Lecture. The floor is yours.

MURRAY L. WEIDENBAUM

Public Service:
The Quiet Crisis

I suspect that when Chris DeMuth conveyed to me the invitation to deliver the annual Boyer Lecture, he would have liked me to deliver a major policy speech. It was not easy to explain that to make a major policy speech you have to make major policy.

It so happens I am out of that business. As I said in Geneva a couple of days ago in an offhand way, I am a monetary has-been. I promptly heard one of my critics has modified that to a monetary never-was.

But if I can't make policy, I can preach—and in signally honoring me today, the American Enterprise Institute has provided an ideal platform to preach about something other than the budget and the dangers of inflation.

That something is what was termed at a conference jointly sponsored by AEI and Brookings last year a quiet crisis. The reference is to the state of the public service in the United States, and especially to the state of the federal government bureaucracy down through the ranks.

I am not thinking of the kind of thing that has captured so much of the attention of this town in recent months—the Irangate affair, the Bork hearings, or the intensity of the examination of the private foibles of those who aspire to national political leadership. Whether or not we think of those events as crises—and I am not at all sure we could hope for a consensus in this room on that point—they are certainly not quiet.

Rather, what those attending the conference last year concluded was becoming a crisis was the unmistakable evidence that is accumulating that government in general, and the federal government in particular, is increasingly unable to attract, retain, and motivate the kinds of people it will need to do the essential work of the republic in the years and decades ahead.

It is a *quiet* crisis because not many people know about it—or care very much about it. That has been true of many political candidates for some years, even though the plain danger is that any administration or Congress will be handicapped in carrying out its policies and programs by a weak civil service. But the situation is just too amorphous, too complicated, too distant for many to get excited about it—that is, until something happens.

Naturally, when a meltdown threatens Three Mile Island, then we want the Nuclear Regulatory Commission to respond pronto—to reassure us that the situation is under control, that their planning and emergency procedures are state of the art, that they have on tap the best talent the country can provide.

Naturally, we are mightily annoyed when incidents, ranging from $100 screwdrivers to hundreds of million dollar anti-aircraft guns that do not work right, keep popping up. They raise questions about the ability of hard-pressed Defense procurement officials to spend literally hundreds of billions of dollars for complicated weapons systems that work reliably, and do it economically.

Naturally, we expect the skies to be safe. Somebody in government is supposed to be smart enough and able enough to ensure that will be true no matter how many planes fill the sky.

And, of course, when the stock market goes bust one day, a lot of sophisticated and aggressive people dedicated to pursuing the opportunities offered by free markets suddenly wonder whether a federal safety net is there—and they want to be able to talk with a knowledgeable and understanding friend at the central bank who is able to get things done.

I realize government for most public employees most of the time is not characterized by such public challenges as these—and it should not be. Much of the best work, by definition, is done away from public view; it is a matter of effective planning and efficient day-by-day administration, out of the sight and out of the minds of the mass of our citizens. That is largely the way it goes, when things are working right. But it does not arouse strong and instinctive support for the bureaucracy among the body politic.

The fact is that in recent years there has not just been indifference toward public service, there has been a distinctly anti-Washington theme in much of our recent political rhetoric, including that of the last two successful presidential candidates. Anti-Washington equates in a lot of minds to antigovernment—and it is very easy to slip from an attitude that what the government is doing is wrong as a matter of policy to an attitude that those who work to implement the policies of their political masters must be wrong-headed and probably incompetent, too.

You may have heard the story about the midwesterner touring Washington with his family. When he got home he was asked to make a luncheon speech about what he learned about government. He did it in two sentences, which I quote: "I visited most of the government agencies in Washington. Thank goodness we don't get all the government we pay for." Then he sat down.

Let's hope that is not the attitude of most citizens. But given the extent of the perception, it is no wonder our best and our brightest in undergraduate and graduate schools have not exactly been excited by the challenge of public service, and especially the federal service. One recent study of 365 seniors at Yale found only one that expressed an interest in a civil service career. If I raise the stakes by looking to one of my alma maters—what is now the Kennedy School of Government at Harvard—only 16 percent of those who completed the two-year master's program in public policy over the past ten years are in a federal career service. Only another 3 percent work on Capitol Hill. If that is the pattern at a graduate professional school that has as its very *raison d'être* training for the public service, we shouldn't expect much enthusiasm to be evident in schools and colleges across the country. And it is not.

Perhaps the most telling indication of a problem lies with the attitudes of those who have been most successful within the civil service. Surveys over the past seven years show that an increasing majority of the Senior Executive Service and the next level below (GS-15s)—essentially the people we count on to manage the machinery of government—say they will not recommend that their own children or other young people emulate their careers.

I don't want to be misunderstood. My impression is that there is still in key agencies a remarkably high level of competence, experience, and dedication at senior levels. That personal observation has been supported by most of the responses to a systematic inquiry that the National Commission on the Public Service (about which I will speak in a moment) made of present Cabinet officers and some agency heads.

But there is also little doubt that talent is thinning, and thinning rather rapidly. The generation entering the federal service in the flush of post–World War II enthusiasm—that is, in the 1950s and early 1960s—is eligible for retirement. Many have taken that option early. The best of the next generation, much too frequently, are leaving even before they reach the top levels—often, not so coincidentally, when their children near college age.

The situation seems to many thoughtful observers to demand that something be done about it. My fond hope is that we can achieve a broad consensus, first on that point, and later on a concrete action program. The opinions of people in this room, experienced in the ways of Washington and with an especially strong interest in seeing coherent public policies effectively implemented, will be crucial to that effort. But success will clearly depend upon broad understanding and support around the country as well.

There is room for skepticism that such a consensus will arise from spontaneous combustion. That is why a small group of Washingtonians—Elmer Staats, Bob Schaetzel, Elliot Richardson, Leonard Marks, and Norman Ornstein from AEI itself—decided about a year ago to create, and seek private funding for, a National Commission on the Public Service. They somehow got Ambassador Bruce Laingen—his own career a model of effective public service—to act as executive director. I was glad to respond to their request that I act as chairman, and I will be spending some of my time over the next year working with other members of the commission. We will collectively analyze the problem, draw on the thinking of citizens all over the country in regional meetings and otherwise, and develop proposals for action. We are aiming to have them available before the next president and the 101st Congress take office. And we would like to have some impact on the political rhetoric before then.

Within the broad rubric of the public service, we will be giving special, but not exclusive, attention to the federal career services. That is important because we sense a particular problem in that area. It is also because other groups are more specifically concerned with the political layer of government, and we will be able to draw upon their work in shaping our conclusions. Plainly, there can be no question of the importance of a president's being able to draw upon a large pool of talented individuals to provide leadership for his programs.

The commission is off to an excellent start in one respect. More than thirty distinguished Americans, knowledgeable and concerned about the problem, have been willing to join the commission. People like Gerald Ford and Walter Mondale, Ed Muskie and John Tower, seven ex-Cabinet officers, business *and* labor leaders, presidents of the Ivy League, the Urban League, and the League of Women Voters all readily responded to our invitation to work together. I think that confirms the sense that the crisis is real, that something ought to be done about it, and that something *can* be done about it.

The variegated political views of members of the commission amply demonstrate another point: it is none of our purpose, as a commission, to deal with the substantive policies of government. As that implies, we will not have any commission position on the size or appropriate scope of governmental activities.

What joins us together is a simple conviction that, whatever the particular policies of an administration and whatever programs are enacted by the Congress, the American public is entitled to have those policies and programs administered as effectively and as efficiently as possible. And that cannot be done without steadily attracting into government a corps of talented administrators and professionals. We need men and women who can work with, and on behalf of, those with political responsibility, but who can also bring relevant experience to bear, provide both expertise and a sense of continuity, and be a source of ideas themselves.

I know there is a contrasting cynical view that some early members of the present administration once propounded: that a weak and ineffective bureaucracy, by its sheer inefficiency, protects our liberties and particularly our economic freedom. The assumption seems to be that relatively incompetent administration of the law will somehow lead to a smaller and less intrusive government.

I am reminded of a true story. A friend of mine hailed a cab in front of the White House to get to Capitol Hill. The taxi driver motioned toward the White House and said, "we ought to abolish the presidency. Waste of money," he said. As they drove past the Supreme Court he made the same suggestion about the nine justices. As he was making change for his passenger in front of the Capitol, the cabbie observed: "And we ought to abolish the House and the Senate. Sheer waste."

This was the last straw for my friend the passenger. "You want to abolish the presidency, the Supreme Court, and the House and the Senate. Who is going to run the country?" he asked.

The cab driver snapped back: "This country can run on its reputation."

Unfortunately, even a good reputation needs the best staff support it can get.

The plain fact is that the federal government today does so many things in total, and so many things that require a high level of professional skill and understanding, that the idea that we can settle for mediocrity in our public services would, in time, become an invitation to mediocrity as a nation.

Even so seemingly a routine process as sending out social security and Medicare payments is an enormous administrative challenge—or nightmare—these days; it involves some 63 million items a month that have to get to the right place on the right day. No private corporation operates on that scale.

Businessmen by their nature will never like regulation. But when they do have to cope with regulations and regulatory problems, I have no doubt that they want to deal with highly competent government professionals who can understand and respond to their problems.

We would all, I presume, cringe at the thought that we might be satisfied to be represented by second-raters overseas or that the secretary of state and others concerned with national security should not have the best in-house advice.

I do not think we are going to stop doing and sponsoring medical research, and we surely don't want that done in a slipshod way—not when we are spending hundreds of millions on cancer research and need to mount an effective attack on AIDS.

And, if I wanted to run a tight conservative administration, cutting back on bureaucracy (in the pejorative sense of that word), I would sure want a bunch of aggressive professional managers in the Office of Management and Budget who knew where the bodies were buried and how to exhume them.

I could go on and on. But surely the argument for

mediocrity cannot be serious, not in the late twentieth century—not in a world of rocketships and nuclear power and atomic bombs, not in a country where the federal government after seven years of the most conservative administration in sixty years still spends over 23 percent of the GNP, not in a city to which an increasingly complex and interdependent world still looks for leadership.

There has been, it seems to me, a more serious political and psychological barrier to achieving more constructive and consistent policies toward the civil service. My observation has been that many new political appointees are suspicious of, if not outright hostile to, the permanent bureaucracy, questioning its ability, its energy, and its purposes. Perhaps Republican administrations have been the most sensitive, suspecting that civil servants tended to be Democrats in favor of expansive government. Once upon a time, that suspicion may have had some basis as a result of the great increase in the bureaucracy in the New Deal days. But a sense of mutual distrust is certainly not unique to Republican administrations.

Over the postwar years, virtually every administration has increased, with congressional acquiescence, the number of political appointments in the executive branch.

Now, I am not totally naive, and I realize civil servants (let's call them bureaucrats for this purpose) can and do develop vested interests in particular programs. Able and aggressive people in any walk of life are not exempt from the temptation to see their own programs, their staff, and their empires grow. They may even do their own discreet lobbying in the Congress.

There have been examples of a self-defeating process when political appointees wall themselves off from career executives—or vice versa. Both sides suffer, and with them effective programs.

But my own direct experience and observation—admittedly mostly at what are considered elite agencies at the center of the government process—have been essentially different. Part of the job of a senior civil servant is to remember; to warn his boss where the potholes lie; to help define what is possible and what is not; to report the facts, good or bad. And the typical professional civil servant also wants to be responsive to strong and clear leadership from an administration of either party. I suspect that responsiveness rests on more than an intellectual appreciation of the fact that the president and his appointees are politically responsible: there is a strong psychological satisfaction in playing on a team that has new ideas and a public mandate, that seems to know where it is going—and is willing to look to the career staff for help.

One apocryphal story captures well that side of civil service ethic.

The Office of Management and Budget is, of course, a central management tool of any administration. Historically it has been the embodiment of neutral competence, and it needs—and tends to attract—the best we have. The story goes that on that day when some unidentified flying objects descend on the mall, when the green men from Mars disembark and nearly all of Washington flees the city, a delegation from OMB will present itself to the Martian leaders asking, "How can we help with the transition?"

Like a good many other government responsibilities, transitions can be a nasty job. But in ordinary circumstances, it helps to have somebody do it right, and a new administration that does not elicit the best from the civil servants is not doing itself justice.

The survey of Cabinet officers and some agency heads that I referred to earlier provides strong support for that thesis. The group surveyed is, of course, almost entirely a group of conservative Republicans. They are now experienced in the federal government and in getting things done. Whatever they anticipated upon taking office, they are close to uniform in expressing respect for the capability, energy, and cooperativeness of senior staff—even if, at the same time, they are worried about losing too many of the best.

Nonetheless, the fact remains that the strong tendency of Democratic and Republican administrations alike to increase the number of political appointments has by now raised their total to over 3,000, and roughly half of those are in jobs that might otherwise be filled by senior career personnel.

The contrast to other mature democracies is startling. West Germany has a grand total of between 50 and 60 "political" appointees—they are political in the sense that the jobs are vulnerable to a change in government, but in fact about half of the incumbents in those positions have been promoted from the civil services. The United Kingdom has about 150 "political" jobs, and France about 400, again with about half of the latter drawn from the civil service. And it may not be entirely accidental that permanent civil servants have generally had high prestige in those countries, with entry-level professional and administrative positions strongly sought by the best students, even though salaries may be little better than here.

Obviously, American civil service traditions are different—arguably more democratic and certainly more open to an influx of new ideas and fresh leadership. But there are clearly costs to so deep a layer of political appointees as well. Quite apart from the loss of experience and continuity in particular jobs, the inexorable effect is that the career paths of permanent civil servants are truncated at lower levels of authority and responsibility. And there is no doubt that able young people in our colleges and professional schools know it. How often have I heard the refrain, "Sure, I'm interested in government, but if I really want to make a difference, I will have to wait until I'm older and get a political appointment."

My guess is that, as middle age approaches, with growing families, rising incomes, and blossoming careers, few of the best of those men and women will in fact be willing to pull up stakes and take a subordinate political appointment. The risk we run is that we will end up with the worst of all worlds—mediocre civil servants and mediocre subordinate political appointees as well.

Moreover, a lot of able young people interested in government seek a job on Capitol Hill where, in their view, they can more quickly be closer to the action. The relative roles of the Congress and the executive in the development and administration of both foreign and domestic policy happens to be a hot issue these days, and I do not want to enter into all that debate here. But one observation is directly relevant.

The enormous proliferation of congressional committee and personal staff inevitably, in my judgment, dilutes the ability of any administration to initiate and control the policy agenda. At the same time, it multiplies the demands on the executive—and ultimately the civil servant—to respond to congressional inquiries, including a great many that are either substantively frivolous or more relevant to a staffer's concerns than that of his congressional boss. Ironically, the more able the congressional staffer, the more pointed the problem. The result seems to be questionable in terms of coherency and consistency of government, and it certainly adds up to another layer of frustration for senior civil servants.

The sensitive area of career-political relationships is bound to be one important subject of inquiry for the commission. It is one of several areas in which our work will overlap with the concerns of other groups, including particularly the work of the Kennedy School on the special problems of the "inners and outers" and the continuing efforts of the Center of Excellence in Government, which draws directly on the experience of past political appointees.

Task forces of the commission are also looking into the important practical problems in the areas of recruitment, retention, and retirement—matters to which the present administration, with the able leadership of Constance Horner, is already devoting attention. It is a sad and ironic fact that good young people with a demonstrable interest in the federal government are today being turned off by enormously cumbersome and time-consuming hiring practices, even when a position is open and an agency is eager to hire. Somehow, it seems clear, a better balance needs to be struck between agency initiative and flexibility in hiring and firing and the need to maintain employment standards and to avoid partisan political pressures across the whole of the civil service.

To discuss intelligently the effectiveness and morale of public servants without considering the question of pay and overall compensation would, of course, be impossible. While it is not the only issue—and not necessarily the most important—the commission inevitably has that subject high on its agenda. It is a well-tilled field, replete with private and public studies, quadrennial commissions, recurrent congressional debate—and strong public impressions.

I confess a strong personal bias. In the private sector, those carrying large responsibilities, willing to take the initiative and bear the consequent risks, are and should be well paid. No civil servant expects the same level of monetary reward. But, when brand new lawyers and business school graduates from the best universities can claim first-year salaries and bonuses in the range of assistant secretaries and under secretaries something is out of kilter.

Looked at another way, to my mind a senior civil servant, in full maturity and at the top of his profession, should be able to send a child to one of our best private colleges without feeling compelled to run into debt or draw heavily upon his slim assets. But as things now stand, he is squeezed in two directions: for almost a decade, salary increases have fallen 40 percent below the inflation rate, while the average tuition at the best private colleges has more than doubled, rising more than twice as fast as inflation.

Now maybe that "Volcker yardstick" is too vague to provide a practical salary guideline. There are, however, more specific questions. Does it, in fact, still make sense to have essentially the same pay scales through the country for the same civil service grades? Is tying top level executive salaries to congressional pay still desirable? Is the present, or any, bonus system effective? Is there room for additional specialized career services in government on the model of the foreign service or the Federal Reserve?

Questions like these are old and obvious. But I do believe the commission is in a position to look afresh at the compensation issue for career and political appointees alike—and potentially to marshal support for constructive change.

It is hard in this country to think of a vigorous body of people professionally committed to a career in government without a supporting system of professional education. For years, the best way to train for the public service has been a matter of dispute, and there has been considerable experimentation in some of our leading universities. But I suppose the main overall impression is one of neglect. There are, it is true, over 200 degree programs in public administration around the country. But with a few notable exceptions, they are underfunded small appendages to business schools or political science departments. With four university presidents on board, this, too, is an area where I hope the commission can shed some useful light.

Finally, the public's perception of the public service—and the morale of the public servants themselves—must in the end rest on demonstrated performance up and down the line. Constructive political leadership at the top, crucial as it is, can go only so far; public trust and confidence will have to be earned by competence and integrity, day by day.

Dwight Eisenhower, a superb example of what a public service career can produce, once put the point with characteristic bluntness: "No [civil service] system should be a haven for the few who are incompetent, dishonest, or disloyal. I intend to see the government rid of all such persons . . . . There is no other way to win for the vast majority of competent and devoted public servants the public honor that is due them."

We need to be at least as conscious of the responsibilities of public employees to the body politic as we are of what needs to be done to improve their position. It is a matter of maintaining the highest ethical standards, but it also needs to encompass all those more mundane things involved in delivering the public services with skill and efficiency. In one respect a civil servant should be like a new computer—if he's not "user friendly," we ought to demand a better model.

A large percentage of the people in this room have, at one time or another, served in government, and most of the rest are closely concerned with substantive issues of public policy. I suppose that, in some general way at least, the idea and the ideal of public service strikes a responsive chord.

That was certainly true of those who created the nation more than 200 years ago. The administrations of the Founding Fathers—Washington and Adams, Jefferson and Madison—brought the best and the brightest of their day to this capital. They instinctively recognized, as Alexander Hamilton put it in *The Federalist,* that "a government ill executed, whatever might be the theory, is in practice poor government."

From today's perspective, what strikes one is how intimate was the Washington establishment in those days. From the president to messengers, there were only about 125 executive branch employees located in all of Washington in the first years of the nineteenth century. (Reportedly the working hours were 9 to 3!) There were only between 2,000 and 3,000 people in the entire executive branch throughout the country, mostly devoted to collecting customs and delivering the mail.

Even so, there must have been recruitment problems. A note Thomas Jefferson once sent to a friend took him to task for being unwilling to take on a larger role in national affairs. "There is a debt of service," he wrote, "due from every man to his country, proportioned to the bounties which nature and fortune have measured to him."

Perhaps that sense of *noblesse oblige* is too elitist to fit entirely comfortably in the American tradition. Jacksonian populism reacted against an aristocratic view. Then, through the subsequent decades, the democratic idea of government by the people degenerated into a crude spoils system. It took the assassination of President Garfield by a disappointed office seeker to give birth to a fledgling civil service system. And it was not until the early part of this century, under the leadership of Teddy Roosevelt and Woodrow Wilson, that the idea of public service as a responsibility and a privilege again took hold.

The years of enormous national challenge—depression, war, postwar reconstruction, and preeminent international leadership—made Washington an exciting place to be. I know from personal experience that a lot of young people then looked upon government as a place where they could combine a sense of challenge and service with a sense of personal satisfaction. As late as the beginning of the 1960s, President Kennedy captured that spirit when he told a group of summer interns, "It is my judgment that there is no career that could possibly be open to you in the 1960s that will offer you as much satisfaction, as much stimulus, as little compensation perhaps financially, as being a servant of the U.S. government."

The point on compensation remains wholly valid. But the countervailing zest for public service reflected in his comment sadly sounds dated. Maybe it is partly a sense that government has gotten too big to make an impact, too messy to permit a personal sense of accomplishment, too vulnerable to criticism and attack to offer much in the way of prestige. So our best young people are tempted to follow the action, financial and otherwise, on Wall Street or to use their ingenuity to represent and defend private clients instead of the public interest.

I cannot reconcile that view with a pertinent recent comment by Elliot Richardson. He pointed out that he has "many friends who once held responsible but not necessarily prominent roles in government and who now occupy prestigious and well-paid positions in the private sector—some of them very prestigious and very well paid. Not one finds his present occupation as rewarding as his government service. If they feel this way, so must a lot of others."

Well, maybe people like Elliot and me are getting old—maybe his words are a nostalgic exaggeration; maybe it really is all different today. But I doubt it. I see too many able people in government doing their best in difficult circumstances, certainly with inadequate pay, precisely because there is no satisfaction like having the United States as your sole client.

Amid all the complexities and complications of the late twentieth century, the wishful thinkers are those that think we can make do with the mediocre. There is less room for error in our foreign relations, not more. Technology demands faster responses, not slower, to problems as widely removed as air safety and financial regulation. National security demands that we know how to build military equipment that works and that we can afford. Our very survival may literally depend on how we respond to complex threats to our environment and to our health.

I have no doubt that public service, now as in the past, can for many provide a strong sense of personal satisfaction. It can, and it will, make a crucial difference in our performance as a nation. No small commission can itself go far toward doing the things necessary to make that potential a reality. But we can sound the alarm, show the flag, and suggest some answers. We mean to do all that.

I am told that there are healthy signs that the public at large is in a mood to demand more from government— more, not in size, but in the sense that they want government to work better. Instead of simply bashing those in Washington, they aim to get a president and a Congress that can deal in a practical and effective way with the evident problems before us.

That president and that Congress—and all the future presidents and Congresses—will need all the help they can get.

Somewhere it is written: "The best shall serve the State." I do not care whether that sentiment ever gets chiseled in stone. But I do think we all should care that it should be part of the American ethic—and that we make it possible for the sentiment to be a reality.

The nation deserves no less.

Francis Boyer Award Recipients

Paul A. Volcker, *Public Service: The Quiet Crisis* (1987)

David Packard, *Management of America's National Defense* (1986)

Jeane J. Kirkpatrick, *The United States and the World: Setting Limits* (1985)

Robert H. Bork, *Tradition and Morality in Constitutional Law* (1984)

Alan Walters, *The British Renaissance 1979—?* (1983)

Hanna Holborn Gray, *The Higher Learning and the New Consumerism* (1982)

Henry A. Kissinger, *The Realities of Security* (1981)

William J. Baroody, Sr., Remembered, Paul W. McCracken, Robert H. Bork, Irving Kristol, and Michael Novak (1980)

Paul Johnson, *The Things That Are Not Caesar's* (1979)

Arthur F. Burns, *The Condition of the American Economy* (1978)

Gerald R. Ford, *Toward a Healthy Economy* (1977)

American Enterprise Institute for
Public Policy Research

0-8447-1385-6